Love's Refuge and Sonnets

By Dudley (CHRIS) Christian

A

Pause For Poetry ©

Publication

Acknowledgement:

Special thanks to my wife, Marilyn Christian for compiling, organizing and finalizing the books of my collections. Her photographic and editing skills were vital to all of my works.

ISBN: 978-0-9877501-0-5

First Edition January 2012
Revised Edition June 2017

Cover Photograph: Oregon Coast © Marilyn Christian

<u>An Opening Word by the Author...</u>

Many people often ask:

"How do you write and do you have to often rewrite your material?"

I have long summed up my answer to the above with the following:

"A Word, the written word, small purveyor of a thought, so like a thought, once thought, cannot be recalled, so too, a word once writ, should need NOT be re-written, for with such licence, we would but change ... the very substance of the thought."

...DNC © 1970

Dudley (Chris) Christian founded and hosted the first and only "PAUSE FOR POETRY" show dedicated solely to the introduction of new and unknown poets and their works. This TV series ran from 1974 to 1985.

Table of Contents

Dear Reader:

Pain, racism, injuries -- even Death sometimes seem to inject themselves into writing when the subject is Humanity. With that in mind, looking back over the past 40 plus years, I found that my collections DO contain also many happy, joy-filled, love blessed and memorable records.

With these I hope to try and temper the impression you may have drawn of me when you were given the glimpse into my life as lain out in my first collection "Judge Me Not Without A Trial."

May this collection serve to further acquaint you with insights of Love, Life and other factual and important periods of my life, as you walk through "Love's Refuge."

Then, take a trip through my 50 plus sonnets, each a photo of a special time. Thank you for coming along on this journey for a fuller understanding of my life.

"Empathy is about standing in someone else's shoes, feeling with his or her heart, seeing with his or her eyes. Not only is empathy hard to outsource and automate, but it makes the world a better place."
        ∽ Daniel H. Pink

Love's Refuge

I Love You, Oh how I love you, if I could own you my life would then be complete, complete not in myself, but in being able to give to you full contentment at all times. To enable me to work for you, to be with you, to comfort you in all your daily occurrences throughout life. I love you not only for what joys you may bring to me, but for that joy which I in my humble attempts may bring to you. As a person my only aims will always be to please you in all ways possible. I would love to give you children, to provide you your meals, to furnish extravagantly the dwelling that I help to create for us, to leave feeling no constraining bonds and to return in the ultimate knowledge that your warm and welcome arms are awaiting me. I would love to awaken each day in your presence and to go to sleep each night in the exuberant glow of your warmth content in the knowledge that in my feeble ways I have brought happiness to you Today.

But, Alas, these desires of mine can not be realized as we are both bound by their racial restrictions elsewhere and must so remain removed one from the other so near yet always conscious of the chasm which must exist between us. We must restrain ourselves, our every feeling, and enjoy that which we ourselves desire not but which we have created. We who created the society in which we live are no longer masters of our creation but have now become as slaves, too afraid of our own ideas of right and wrong, good and evil to enable ourselves to grasp that happiness and joy of life which should be our first and ultimate goal of living. We condemn ourselves before we have undertaken to establish proof of our guilt and thus we live in our empty tomb-like existence.

So my love, whom I love above all else, before myself and far beyond the reaches of society conscience or beliefs, one whom I love with no concern or question as to whether it be good or bad right or wrong living only because I am and by so being I am able to love you. Therefore my love feel free forever to come to me at morning, noontime or the dead of night come to me for help, comfort, understanding or any of the pleasures which I may be able to give freely to you with no attachments save the full joy which is mine in return for so giving. Ask of me and it shall be thine, need me and I will appear, seek me and I shall come at my topmost speed to render to you all within my power that you desire.

Let me remain within that secret area of your mind wherein only you can enter, and then the world, and society, and wrong and evil, can never reach out to destroy me or remove me from your presence. Then my love, I too shall be content in this knowledge that I have been afforded the ultimate pleasure of giving you a taste of life's happiness and contentment by being no more or less than that which I so desire to be... YOUR REFUGE.

~Dudley (Noel) Christian

Note: "Love's Refuge" © 1971 is available as an 11" x 17" poster. Contact author at www.dncsite.ca

Alone Nonetheless Again

Meanings to an empty life she brought

And having fast established worth

Reached out and grasped my heart

In grip of soft sweet woman's touch

Leaving naught but joy in memories

Yet alone nonetheless again am I . . .

Naught with but her fond memories

Yet 'tis her smile. . . her voice I feel

Veering ever through my darkest hour

Opening light again to enter there

Night's darkness. . . to suppress its powers

Night's loneliness to fill with warmth

Evernear her love it comforts me...

But... alone nonetheless again am I

Among My Treasures

The sands of fleeting time flows by

The thin icy sheet of hope melts down

The warmth of Winter's Sun shows false

As Cold and drab the World becomes

The silence of the passing nights

No longer by thy sweet breath breaks

As dreams like visions of the mind

Pack up their things and onwards fly

Yet thru it all the Heart hangs on

In everlasting pain of thought

In seeking searching loneliness

In Quest as always for its own

Yet as the Silent hands of time

Takes on its cold and clammy job

To try and ease the passing pain

The selfsame pain once more returns

What then the heart does for its joy

When all its hopes and dreams depart

It lives in treasured memories still

As all hearts do when love departs

It reaches out in useless grasp

To grip the hologram-like hand of love

To watch it pass and reappear

On other shores in other lands

And still the lonely Heart it knows

That hope alone is all that's left

That love itself a fleeting fancy is

But passing by but to warm itself.

Alas, alas there then is naught

Naught but the warmth one does create

To hold the hope to keep the life

To onwards go thru life each day

Oh fool, you fool, you fool to dream

To be again in love's trap caught

You will again but feel the pains

As payment for ecstasy you sought

For I, yes I, I love, am cold

And hard, unfair, unfeeling too

I live but to take hearts like thine

And crush their feelings into dew

And as that dew the good Earth wets
When from their eyes it falls like rain
I relish then the pain they've shared
Pain which new hearts will give again

Alas, alas, Dear heart of mine... adieu
The voice of love of life and truth
Has spoken and we it must heed
'Tis useless to hang on to naught
When all we sought has passed it seems
So friend adieu, dear Heart adieu
Cause not my pain thy life to touch
Beat on again mechanically
Knowing well this time was just too much
Goodbye farewell we live and love
We find and win and also lose
But we in this eternal void
Of loneliness just cannot choose
So grasp shall ever we forever
When opportune it passes by
Tho knowing always that the end
Will see me alone and see thee cry
Goodbye, dear friend, dear heart goodbye...

18/Oct/1986

Like Two Angels from Heaven

Like two angels from heaven descending,

To brighten a dark world of grey

To lighten the heart and to offer

Hope to go on life's way

So soft, warm and welcome

They sit there,

In splendour of times that's gone,

So in innocent childhood they smile,

So full of life and oh so warm,

Whoever could think but to love them,

With feelings deep tender and true,

Whoever could think to harm them,

It rests not in our thoughts so to do,

Nothing doth seemeth to sway now,

Their sweet soft and angelic smiles,

While their voices echoes like music,

To soothe our pains of lost pride,

Yes we too can look and consider,

The ways of a woman in youth,

Before there enters her memory

The pain of this earth and its truth,

Oh why has our universe slipped so,

To shackle condemn and destroy,

Why let we their innocence suffer,

Which is beauty to each girl and boy,

Consider cold world of such sorrow,

How happy and free we could be,

If only you spoilt not our innocence,

If only life's greed we'd not seen

I Shall Call Thee...

I shall call thee at the borning

Of a dark and dismal day

Or maybe at the creeping

As night our way wends its way

Just to see that ray of sunlight

Fall again here from your face

To but bright anew my living

Lend its beauty to this place

Then tho I'll but have listened

As that's all of which I've choice

You will brighten, warm and cheer me

When I call to hear your voice

Then tho not as lover but just friend

My heart will live and sing again

You Ought To

A positive force – Humanity
A negative charge – Eternity
Together forms a whole
One cannot with the other gone
Exist so on its own
Life deals us little reasons
As well as a cross to bear
But for our good or bad times
Love sends someone to share ...

You ought to let somebody love you
Take care, support, protect you
Look for, long for, desire you
For life is not lived – alone.

Love can't be substituted
Nor traded for work nor duty
It cannot be full buried
Under parenthood's great demand

It will not be quietly stifled
Nor riled when daily trifled
But remains in obstinacy
Clear as lines etched in your hand ...

You ought to let somebody love you
Take care, support, protect you
Look for, long for, desire you
For life is not lived – alone.

Then reach out and respond now
To that which offers you love
Tho strange may be its trappings
You must trust and try to grasp
One touch it may assure you
Bring down the wall that's 'round you
Give life a brand new meaning
If you but surrender to its clasp...

You ought to let somebody love you
Take care, support, protect you
Look for, long for, desire you
For life is not lived – alone.

So let somebody love you
Life is so empty all alone
Let somebody love you
Let somebody love you
Let somebody love you
Before its too late

(mer) 20/9/91

Let Me Sit and Gaze

Let me sit and gaze

In the eyes I am beholding

The love of time that could be mine

If her heart did not start aching

The kind of love I am searching for

So deep and warm—longlasting

The heart that's true to only me

And never will deceive me

It's the kind of love I'll one day find

If I can just keep looking

Let me sit and gaze

In wonder -- amazed

At the hand that I am holding

At the lips I press to mine again

In a kiss for which I'm longing

In the eyes that do seem warm and true

That holds the world and all its sorrows

Let me sit and gaze

In this foggy haze

While in my mind I ponder

All the days of old that passed me by

While she sat and so did wonder

If I'd ever see her love for me

And realize the strain she's under

Let me sit and gaze in my daily haze

In the eyes I am beholding

Let me sit and gaze

Let me sit and gaze

Let me sit and gaze -- forever

Thoughts of Love

Thoughts of Love

Which this pen writes

Will soothe the heart

To fear give flight

Will pass to hearts

Which lonely ache

Worlds of love's comfort

For Love's own sake

Only then can they

These thoughts of Love

Be passed to convey

True thoughts of Love

To you

With Love

On this your very special Day

Everyone Knows Lonely Days

Everyone knows lonely days

Life's like that at times

Ain't really much that anyone

I've known can to it do

Nor would we try to it correct

Ever more its so

18-Jun-80

The Girl in the Barroom

She walks along life's lonely street

With head bowed low and thoughts so deep

No one would think she'd ever cared

That poor drunk girl just sitting there

Her eyes and face they tell of time

And ages past that she has spent

The marks of youth no longer bides

To hide her hurts and pains and fears

Soft slowly to the barroom clerk

She signals for a glass of gold

A liquid that will ease the thoughts

And dim the memory she must hold

Across the room her glance it goes

To rest with lingering look upon

A face that once she loved in vain

A man who from her now is gone

She holds no grudge against the ways

That fate has changed her early years

She feels no malice for the wasted days

She feels now nothing but her tears

Within her heart she cries once more

And whispers soft a little prayer

She'd gladly run if his arms would hold

A welcome signal insignificant there

'Tis been four hours now and she

Has hardly strength to sit and wait

The golden liquid she drank so free

Fast now her pride it will abate

Oh little girl your loves and dreams

In haste you tried life's road to run

But hurt and pain and time now seems

To 'ave shown by Patience only is it done

If There Exists Still in This World

If there exists still in this world

Such a thing dear as real love

I think I'd know that very girl

If I could find her now

I do believe that I would see

It resting in her eyes

I'd see it in her thoughts of me

Hear it in her tender sighs

And far beyond the days that be

I could freely show each day

The way that her love affects me

In every way each day

So if your eyes speak out so true

'Tis what I see in your heart it's you

Be My Love Forever

Be my love forever

Ever by my side

Varying in love never

Eternally my bride

Reliving each experience

'Long life's dreary roads

Why? Because I love you

You and you alone

Take me for your lover

Home to my heart please come

Others second never

My one and only one

Soon our life'll be over

Over here on this earth

No more parting ever

With God who gave us birth

Wait Somewhere Safe for Me

Wait somewhere safe for me
Wherever you go
Take care of you for me
Cause I'll miss you so
And whether your wanderings
Take you far away
Wait somewhere safe for me
I beg you today

Wait somewhere safe for me
With a smile and a song
I'll think of you tenderly
As time passes on
And one day again we'll meet
On the shores of the sea
Wait somewhere safe for me
Wherever you be

Wait somewhere safe for me
Though nights will be cold
With thoughts of your warmth
I'll be warm till life's over
Then I'll return once more
To where you're waiting for me
And my life will have been content
So... PLEASE
Wait somewhere for me

Come to Me Dear in the Morning

Come to me dear in the morning
Come to me dear at set of Sun
Come to me dear in the cool of evening
Or when the hour of midnight has begun
Come to me dear in the morning
Or when starlight fills the evening sky
Come to me wherever you may be
But darling always always come to me
Come to me when Summer's Sun is shining
Come to me when Winter's snowflakes fall
Come to me when Autumn's leaves are falling
Or when Spring wakes the flowers one and all
Come to me when wars and famine threaten
Come to me at home at work or play
Come to me wherever I may be
But darling always always come to me
Come to me when your heart is broken
Come to me when all your plans seem lost
Come to me recalling words I've spoken
Still come to me regardless of the cost
I will always always love you only
You will always be my Darling Love
Come to me and mend my poor heart broken
Come to me wherever you may be
But Darling always always come to me

Leaving Me With a Heart of Love

Leaving me with a heart of love

On a day I'll never forget

Right before my eyes appearing now

Really filled with sorrow and regret

And though I can only tell her that I love her

I know I'll miss her when she's away

Never caring to find another

Ever waiting for her returning day

Why did I fall in love again?

Only perhaps my heart to have broken

Or will it work to make us twain

Dedicated to these vows solemnly spoken

Do you really love me now forever

United always hereafter to be

Do you promise to leave me never

Loving -- caring trusting only me

Each of us must make this promise

Yet we're free so far I know

Not doubtful of each others promise

Just content to love each other so

Cherishing deep love we've found -- together

Holding on ever to what we've got

Reaching never for another

Intent only on our chosen lot

Someday clinging to each other

Taking with the good the bad

Interested in happiness for each other

Always cheerful tho life may be sad

Never caring never sharing any love aside

Today At Work There Was a Man

Today at work there was a man

Who'd never worked with us before

A man who'd seen fifty years if he'd seen three

But I hung my head in sorrow at the story that he told

For it reminded me so much of me

For the story that he told was but an olden tale of woe

Where he had had a woman fine and true

Of how he often hurt her, of how he loved her still

Of how he'd left her all alone and blue

He said she was a woman so kind so sweet and good

Who tried in every way to please her man

And tho at times he'd be long gone

She always by him stood

Thru all the years the bottle ruled her man

He told of how not long ago he'd come to realize

The torment and the torture she did bear

Of how now tho it broke his heart –

He'd finally set her free

For her to find contented love somewhere

He'd wished her well and left her

With all that she might need

As far as earthly goods and treasures go

But just like me he'd found too late

His love was all she craved

And like a fool he'd let his true love go

I knew the story well friend for so I too had gone

Not realizing the sorrow life can hold

'Til I'd lost the only one I loved cause I carried on

With every new and willing face I did behold

Accidentally On Purpose

Accidentally on Purpose

I chanced to meet you

Accidentally on Purpose

Things happened as they do

You crossed by the streets

Of my lonely heart

Bringing them light

Bringing them joy

Your warm embrace filled me I know

With a warm touch

A glow

Wheresoever I go

So until we meet again

On some other day

I'll wait in the hope of saying one day

Accidentally on Purpose

Tho it's been a long time

I've missed you li'l Darling

And wished you were mine

Mine to be held here by my side

Mine to be cared for forevermore

'Til I am tired and pass from this land

To have you beside me

To hold your hand

Tho it has all been

Just a quick dream

Accidentally on Purpose

It was so it seems

Yet ne'er will I regret

One minute of that time

When Accidentally on Purpose

For awhile you were mine

I'm Sorry

I'M SORRY

That fate had us meet so

So late in life for me

I'M GLAD

That time stood still awhile

And you stopped awhile by me

I'M HAPPY

To have known you Dear

To have held you near and warm

I'M SAD

Because now that you're gone

You'll never more be mine

But I'll keep a memory

Of times I dreamed

Of things I hoped

Of a friendship

Warm and true

Perhaps again in life we'll meet

Until then friend I'll say

May God smile with Love on You

I Know Now

It's not improbable I know now
But not impossible I know now
It's not unlikable I know now
But not unthinkable I know now
That my love for you
Will last —— Forever

For as long as the stars shine above
Thru all the dreary winter years of life my love
I will always see the Sun with you as my wife
My love my love
It's unbeatable I know now
Perhaps unreachable I know now
Quite unsearchable I know now
But not in-understandable I know now
The way that I love you

When winter years draw nigh
You won't have to cry
Cause I'll always be there by your side
With a love divine
Truest you could ever find
As young as warm as the day
You first were my bride

Today At Work I Sat Alone

Today at work I sat alone

Without a thought serene

I somehow could not think alone

Or so to me it seemed

I looked afar for someone new

To talk or chat awhile

But alas I see if it's not you

There's little reason for me to smile

So lonely I do sit here now

Intent to this day see through

Content that on the 'morrow somehow

I'll spend some time with you

The sea is bright the waves all calm

The Sun so cheerily shine

But still in the crowd alone I am

Since you I just can't find

Yet sleep on sweet dream so far

Tho away e'er near you'll stay

Life made us to live as we are

Life'll give us soon our day

One day our nights will never end

One night our dreams we'll see

One time forever with you I'll spend

One time you'll belong to me

Today at work I sat alone

Without a thought serene

I thought my dear of you alone

You're the vision of my every dream

That's Jody

A kiss a smile a warm embrace -- that's Jody

A laugh a pout an angel's face -- that's Jody

A woman with all the charms

To cradle love there in her arms

And hold a man safe from harm -- that's Jody

A frown a thought a question deep -- that's Jody

A devil awake an angel asleep -- that's Jody

The only girl in all the world

Who could make come true the dreams I hold

And never realize to me she's gold -- that's Jody

That's Jody a girl that I know -- that's Jody

She puts my mind in a misty whirl so -- that's Jody

She's taught me things in a few days

That's changed my living and my ways

To a wonderment of joy for always -- that's Jody

So I'll wait for someday she'll understand --

that's Jody

And return to the arms of her loving man --

that's Jody

She'll then return here to stay

Never more to turn away

Changing back my night to day --

that's Jody

Hello I Found This — I Love You

Hello I found this — I love you

Hello I found this — I love you

I've also no one to talk to

So hello I found this — I love you

===========

On a quiet August in the city

Where last Autumn an old man walked alone

A lonely orphan's face by a window

Lay pressed against the window's pane

The little girl was regretting

How this Summer it would soon be gone

And tearfully remembering last Autumn

When an old man's friendship she had known

===========

She recalls the tiny piece of paper

She'd watched him lift and read with trembling hands

Hoping he'd understand the crayoned writing

Look up and see her tiny waving hand

And he did — and he waved

And everyday thereafter he'd come

to exchange gifts and talk and smile

And she was happy — and he smiled

Then came the first day of June and he didn't show

And she waited — tho inside she knew —

she would never see him again

===========

Now a big car pulls up to the home

A man and lady walk quickly up the way

Coming in they ask about the little girl who wrote

This crayoned written note they bare

No one seems to know so she comes forward

Timid — shy — and scared as she can be

And she sees her crayoned note on which he'd written

Hello I love you — for you from me

===========

Inside the letter given was a picture of the old man

With whom she'd spent such happy hours

Telling her of a great flower bedecked mansion

He had left her for her very own

And he asked that she take her young mute friend

To live with these people once orphans just like you

Then on the tear-stained end he told her

That long ago he'd been an orphan too

Goodbye glad I found this I love you

Goodbye glad I found this — I'll miss you

But now you'll always have someone to talk to

So goodbye — glad I found this — I love you

Goodbye glad I found you — I love you

Laugh With Me

Laugh with me

Walk with me

Take my hand let's move

Since you know

The road to go

Take my hand let's move

You are my inspiration

You awaken my ambition

You bring me fully alive yes you do

You control my pessimisms

You hold to my optimisms

You keep me alive yes you do

You can sing so sing on

You can smile so smile on

You bring joy to me it's true

Your voice is like the angels

Your hair soft to my touch

So clean and so lovable are you

Laugh and walk and lead me

Inspire awaken or console me

Condemn or sing or smile with me

Forever 'long life's roads

Bring joys of pains or sorrows

Or soft warm tender caress

But if in it all

You bring it to me

I'll remain content you to possess

Thanks for Your Message

Thanks for your message of last night

Which came from the heavens above

It came on the tail of a star bright

It told me I needed your love

The rain tried to drown out your message

The wind tried to blow it astray

But God knew the message was for me

So on a star bright he sent it my way

Star bright you're moving so swiftly

Leaving a trail in the sky

Take back this message to Gracie

Tell her I love her in reply

My heart cries for you on this ocean

Each time a star it shoots by

So send me your love and devotion

On a star shooting cross the blue sky

I'll Bless You With My Wishes

I'll bless you with my wishes

And wish you only well

Within my heart forever

Your memory will dwell

Tho I may never own you

One thing I'll surely know

I'll bless you with my wishes

Wherever I may go

I'll bless you with my wishes

And ask the God above

To reach into your heart dear

And place there true true love

Love that is all enduring

For me and me alone

While I bless you with my wishes

And wish you were my own

I'll bless you with my wishes

And as the years go past

We'll recall our happy days

And let the sad ones pass

I'll worship you and love you

For as long as I shall live

And bless you with my wishes

And all the love that I can give

I'll bless you with my wishes

And when our life is through

In death I'll rest contented

Cause Darling I've loved you

And when the great great Father

Calls us to arise

I'll bless you with my wishes

There beyond the skies

She Comes to Me Each Morning

She comes to me each morning

And she whispers soft -- I love you

She takes my hand and presses it

While close beside me warm, she nestles

Then in my heart there burns anew

That flame that only she can kindle

And all my life is happy then

That's some of the reasons I love you

You are the one that touches warm

My thoughts 'n' memories when I see you

You bring to me warm tenderness

That only comes when you I caress

Let me nestle in your arms

Remain there safe from all my harms

And ne'er feel alone or lonely

Then as you feel my heart by yours

You'll come to know I love you truly

So don't forget me whatever you do

Remember forever, that I still love you

No fears and no regrettings

In life will you ever know

For I'll be here beside you

Whither soever you may go --

So take your time and think love

When we two are apart

How long now I have loved you

Now you know you own my heart

Forever and forever I'll be true

Waiting for your coming to me

True and ever in love with you

I need you ever near by me

True and ever waiting

For your coming to me

Tho Times May Be Unstable

Tho times may be unstable --

You'll wonder a lot about me

Remember me and why I love you

Love You?? Why do I love You GRACE

For giving me the feelings of a man,

feelings that circumvent life's bitterness

and shows me that our God is real in each of us

A feeling that destroys in me

the spirit of wandering and lust

And instills one of security and trust --

A feeling which gives me strength to go on each day

with a belief in myself which conquers fear,

A feeling which gives me delight in all I am able to do

if it in some way will add to the expressions

of my love for you

Why do I love you GRACE I love you for the joys of life,

a happy home and the warmth of infant love

which you made possible by your gift to me of a child,

The little patter of footsteps or the early chatterings of a

voice yet not discernable

The awakening smile of warmth around scattered teeth,

the beauty of love innocent and true

in gleaming worshipful eyes,

The annoyances and pranks which make my days

worth living and my home a happy place to come to

all add to my reasons for loving you as I do

Why do I love you?? Over all that I have said above,

over all the others

which across my path life has scattered,

over all the hurts and pains,

over all the little things which makes life's burdens

heavy on my shoulders,

over all that life may deal to me,

over not only my friends

and all earthly possessions but also over myself

I love you for being mine, for being yourself,

for accepting me as I am, was, or will be, for living

and learning in your innocence

the bitterness and hardships of life

yet sharing them joyously with me as no other has done,

could do, or shall ever by God's help be allowed to do

Above before and always tho Grace

I love you for yourself

and for being yourself I Love You

Every Night At Dark I Take

Every night at dark I take

A walk out in the city

To try to find what I was meant to do

But then I start to thinking

Of our spoilt and harried life

And the misery and hurt we both go thru

Now I have found — other arms that soothe me

As she kisses me and holds me warm and tight

And tho she looks a lot like you she's oh so different

That's why your ring hurts my finger each night

I had hoped that we could try to find a new life

In a business way since love has passed us by

But e'en in that you have shown no interest

Still it breaks my heart to see you sit and cry

You never really grew to be a woman

I should have see that clearly from the start

Like a toy you used my pride

'Til you hardened me inside

I've become a shell with a broken heart

Now I have found — other arms that soothe me

As she kisses me and holds me warm and tight

And tho she looks a lot like you she's oh so different

That's why your ring hurts my finger each night

Towering O'er the Expanse...

Towering o'er the expanse of a sunlit beach

O'er the bodies of sunworshippers laying there

Melting in a reaching warm embrace

Enjoying full the moments short they could share

Letting pent-up feelings, theirs, ooze out

In sweet perspiration their two bodies joining

So needful of each others cooling body touch

So needful of each others inner warmth

And even more of each others deep understanding

Who are these dismal shadows, souls apart

Entities of spirit, thought or matter firm

Consider yet the blackberries green nearby

And the songbirds high above the trees

Reaching each to sing or to tell these two

Ecstasy will be reached in time by you

When the green berries turn a richer black

Evening time a brighter reddish sheen takes on

Don't despair, lips so cold will again turn warm

On and on and on for those who care...

I Don't Need You

I don't need you for health

For the doctor says I'm healthy

I don't need you for wealth

For my accounts show I'm wealthy

I don't need you for company

For company's easily found

I don't need you to pick me up

For I haven't been down

I don't need you for house or name

For warmth or strength or fame

I don't need you for intellect

For my brain is far from lame

I've been around this world and seen

All that life holds in store

Along its length across its width

You can offer me no more

Woman oh woman oh woman

I've had the best that be in life

I've seen the worst of days

I've passed my time in joy and strife

I've tried each of life's ways

I've built I've bought and I've torn down

Just to once more start anew

The fallacies which life throws around

'Bout loves hopes dreams and you

I need you not for anything

'Neath Hell nor in Heaven above

You can give or offer me no more

Woman than your sweet free love

So if you hold your values set

So high above beyond my means

In waiting for terms to be met

Which fit your feminine schemes

Remember that whilst you're waiting

I'll find someone who's willing free

To give and share with no bartering

LOVE the one thing you could give me

If Ever a Man Did Reach

If ever man did reach for heaven

To pick himself a star

Or ever bee did seek a flower

To by its fragrance be o'er-powered

If life be long and time persists

Our paths to keep apart

Then I in dreams and I in thoughts

Will keep you in my heart

If you pass o'er this time of life

Unknowing of the pain

Then you will stand as always love

Desired loved unblamed

For how could heavens majesty

E'er cast thy life upon

A single penance for a sin

When it knows you've done no wrong

But ah alas if you did know

And seek my heart to break

Be careful of the times of life

Which revenges each mistake

For tho afar perhaps forever

You stay a lovely dream

And tho your hand I may ne'er hold

I'll love you just the same

But take not love as it here stands

To be words of lust or woe

'Tis but a warm and feeling good

Appearing when you by I go

And far away and pure and chaste

My love will long for you grow

For in years to come you may seek to find

A distant love which does so silently grow

Why Do I Love Thee

Why do I love thee

Is the question of time

So let me recall to you

These past days of mine

I love you for yesterday

And for all of its joys

The pleasures you brought me

And e'en my little annoys

I love you for making it

A day filled to the brim

And for being so considerate

To my each tiny whim

I love you for last week

Tho it now seems long gone

I recall it so clearly

Each night day and dawn

I remember my troubles

When I felt so let down

Yet your consoling assurance

You kept ever around

I love you for last year

Tho it now has been spent

With many a smile and a tear

And an occasional repent

Yet I recall that thru it all

You always stood by me love

You've made my Earth a Heaven

You're a treasure from above

But most of all I love you

For the day that you were born

Without your waiting for me

I ne'er could've gone on

So beautiful yet sheltered

You were waiting patiently

To be my life's love ever

And that's why I love thee

You've Taken All My Trials

You've taken all my trials

My sins and sorrows borne

I've done so little in return

I know oft I've let you down

Yet your heart 'twas forgiving

Your love so warm and true

As I look back at myself I think

What without you would I do

I never pay attention strong

To all your wants and pains

I seem so self engrossed in life

That all else second-place doth seem

I strive within to build a world

Wherein safe I may abide

But deep inside I just can't live

Without you by my side

So thank you dear for caring

In the many ways you do

Thank you too for sharing

The love I know so true

Thank you for just love being

The one that to me is life

I've loved you once

I love you still

My dearest darling wife

I've Hurt Too Many Times

I've hurt too many times before

Not to rush headlong into the same mistake again

I've seen too many empty eyes

Not to open mine and appraise carefully

I've seen too many Suns set

Without even a Moon to take their place

Not to be suspicious as a day nears its end

I've seen too many loves fade and disappear

Not to pull my coat around me

And turn my back on a world

Wherein nothing seems to last

I guess what I want to say is

Hold on just a little bit tighter

I love you so much that I don't want to let you go

When Life's Passions...

When life's passions all surround you

And your thoughts a journey takes

To return and find you waiting

For life's end and for peaces sake

As you ponder on the fullness

Of lives other you have known

And the lone and bitter emptiness

Which seems to portray your own

Then recall the Sun bright shining

And a beach so warm and white

Or a moon bright 'nough for reading

On a warm midwinter's night

Too recall warm soft arms tightly

Wrapped your body full about

As wet welcome lips press fully

To sup full from your own mouth

Kisses flow and love encounters

All of which your life has held

Warmth and love and understanding

Once within your grasp you held

Temper then thy lonesome feelings

As life's passions now by you pass

And hold onto fonder memories

When you enjoyed it in times past

Let the love and let the laughter

Which you crave but cannot touch

Bring back the days of yore hereafter

And ease your heart which pains so much...

She Sneaked Up On Me

She sneaked up on me

She touched my fingers light

I glanced aside and I beheld

Her lovely eyes so bright

Her face so young uplifted

Did search mine deep and dark

So shy, afraid so questioning

Her moves, her voice, her laugh

I turned and pulled her softly

Until my arms therein

I held the vision of my dreams

Her body pressed warm and thin

So soft in sweet surrender

So warm and good to touch

So much a woman yet so innocent

This young girl I'd wanted oh so much

"I'm yours" she said "forever

Take me now and let me see

The heaven that I've ached and longed for

Come make a woman out of me

Do to me all that you've wanted

Show to me what I've missed in life

I'm not scared nor coy any longer

I'm safe secure now I'm your wife

You've waited in so great patience

Until I had grown to be

A fully blown and ready woman

You've been so patient love with me

I too have wanted you but waited

Not for reason other than I feared

That I would in some way disappoint you

That I might fail cause love I'd not shared

But I know that I was foolish

You'll ne'er leave my side love again

I've come to trust and want you darling

So help me now I'm still a virgin"

I knew the ecstasy of life's heaven

As closer she her body pressed

As we left this world to slowly enter

That blissfulness of love's contentness

Thank You You Brought It All Back

I'd forgotten how much hurt feels
When someone says goodbye
Thank you, you just brought it all back
I'd forgotten what a broken heart really means
Thank you, you just brought it all back
I'd forgotten how lonely lovelessness is
Thank you, you just brought it all back
You've renewed all my memories
Of what I'd hoped was all past
So thank you, you brought it all back

You brought it all back to the forefront
Every pain each hurt and each tear
Each bittersweet memory of parting
Which I'd suffered thru so many years
You opened my world back to living
Then dashed me the hardest in fact
Tore me to bits and to pieces
Thank you you brought it all back

Thank you, you brought it all back
All the sorrows and hurts left behind
Thank you, you brought it all back
All the memories and unrest of mind
Thank you, you brought it all back
You've renewed all my memories
Of what I'd hoped was all past
Thank you, you brought it all back
Yes thank, you brought it all back

Sonnets

Just a few verses of thought, on the four uppermost subjects in our everyday life, and on our minds. Also included, are a few selections from a collection of more than 600 bits of poetic verse in sonnet form.

I hope this collection will thrill you enough to encourage you to read further works of mine, which started at the age of 15 and spanned the world, in travels and experiences.

Still working, writing, traveling and thinking of you all, with my usual pen and paper, looking at you.

~ Dudley (Chris) N Christian

Introduction

Oh friend or curious reader
Tho we have never met
I've tried herein to temper
The many things I've met
I try to understand you
That you me too may know
Then as equal human beings
You and I may closer grow
It's useless to be hateful
When Pollution kills us all
So let Love be yours faithfully
And in Life you'll ne'er crawl
... For 'tis better for man to live
Than die with so much to give.

Extra Thought ~ 1

In humble ways you started
And honestly did grow
'Til truth of toil unended
Did your ambitions show
Content not to be stagnant
You built and tried again
You've no cause to be repentant
For to man you were a friend
Now at last you have seen
In this your finest goal
Your life's every aim and dream
Which you so long did hold
May your prosperity continue
The world needs honest men like you.

Extra Thought ~ 2

I've heard as I did wander
Of many a rhyme and ode
To things from far out yonder
To animals and birds old
To some fast fading rendezvous
With shattered hopes and dreams
To lovelorn hearts sad and blue
Lost in all their every scheme
I've seen the words fast written
As a river which overflowed
Smashing or being smitten
As it goes down life's long road
So like their dedications sad or true
I send on this ode my love to you

Extra Thought ~ 3

Oh my heart cries like a flowing river
As my sorrows like Lemmings multiply
For I know that I must go on forever
While you from me like swallows fly
Yet within the deepness of my bosom
Beats a heart that cries just for you
While I sail alone lost on this ocean
With all my hopes and dreams of you
My solace I do find while sailing
Upon the salty seas I travel on
Dreaming of one for whom I'm pining
One that has from me forever gone
Still I live hoping to some day learn
That to my side once she'll return

Extra Thought ~ 4

If life should e'er of me demand
To be your steadfast stone
To see me e'er by your side fast stand
You'll ne'er dear stand alone
Or if it should be hard to me
And keep us ever apart
Regret of knowing you, you won't see
Ever enter in my heart
For the times I did hold you near
Will be my future life
Tho a memory may be all we share
Henceforth in our short life
But just to have know you and loved you
Will ever bring me joy in all I do.

Extra Thought ~ 5

Over the blue and misty ocean
There lies a railroad line
Which is alive with motion
It seemeth all the time
That railroad has a train
On which my girl did go
Leaving me in lonely pain
In a life of grief and woe
I've lived on oh so all alone
Without a place to be
My life it has meaningless grown
That's why I went to sea
To try to lose my memories
Of the days you spent with me.

Love ~ 1

Smoke is a passing cloud
Produced by heat they say
Love is a feeling proud
Which warms your every day
Love is a cloud at times
Which o'ershadows all our plans
With a smokelike haze it binds
Men and women in many a land
Yet like the smoke of fires
Its blown upon the wind
Putting some to heights e'en higher
Casting others down again
Yet like the air we're helpless
Loves existence ever to resist.

Love ~ 2

Yet there are many that do try
In their feeble futile ways
Regretting if it passes by
In their latter lonely days
They grasp the Earth's treasures
With hand and foot and teeth
Forgetful of giving pleasure
To the lonely hearts they meet
Then childless and so loveless
They spend their autumn years
With no tender words or soft caress
To hold back their bitter tears
Alas Oh Love it seems again
Another battle of life you win.

Love ~ 3

But are you really happy
In fact are you content
Bringing to hearts unhappy
Life's blessing in full content
Or is it cause you're lonely
Or have known sorrow too
That you live onwards only
To remove our grief and blue
Then tell me if you can love
How do you your riches share
That tho each one knows full love
You still have lots to spare
It is a mystery you give
Which makes the world good in to live.

Love ~ 4

Flowing like the sea of time
Which flows by every land
You touch upon the heart sometimes
Of every living man
You open wide the gates within
Which seals his heart with walls
Laying out the golden stair again
Each time you help him fall
You play your music sweetly
Upon his thin heart strings
And bring to him completely
The peace for which he sings
Then you may stay for many a day
Or else in haste you run away.

Love ~ 5

What game is it you're playing
While a heart in sorrow cries
What story part you're saying
Is your story part all lies
What is it that you're after
As a broken heart you mend
Do you bring it joy and laughter
Just to see it break again
Or is this but your duty
To seek out and destroy
Whilst clothed in such beauty
Do you really jest and toy
Or are your notions stable
Staying always long as able.

Love ~ 6

O'er mountain vale and ocean
I've traveled searching all
For a love with true devotion
Which for my heart doth call
A love that like the sunrise
Is constant warm and true
A love that I can truly prize
In all I undertake to do
And such a love you gave me
The first time you did smile
I felt your heart open wide to me
That I might come inside
Building there a place so true
Living warm henceforth with you.

Love ~ 7

My plans are now realities
My dreams have all come true
My life has meaning now you see
'Cause I love and am loved by you
My thoughts are bright and shiny
My rainbows never go
My aspirations are you only
In my darkness you're my glow
You fill my every pastime
I think of naught but you
I feel I've found true love this time
But do you feel so too
Without your true reply
Inside I'll ever wonder why.

Love ~ 8

True love it has no fear
Or so a great man said
But it shows how little he cared
If he feared not it could go dead
He mayhap spoke of feelings
Which lies deep down inside
With no thought in his writings
To life and death and pride
Or mayhap I did misunderstand
The feelings which he knew
So I ask forgiveness from this man
If his "true love" love is like you
For greater fear I cannot say
Than the fear you too may go away.

Love ~ 9

Again to you I humble call
In deepest woe anew
My hopes and plans have tumbled all
As in fear I turn to you
Last nigh in dreams I held you close
Pressed to my heart so warm
Caressed the one I love the most
But awoke with empty arms
I gathered all my foolish pride
And cast it far away
I've come back love here to your side
E'ermore in your arms to stay
Hoping that my love I'll learn
To love you more as you do yearn.

Love ~ 10

Forgive a foolish heart I say
And cast me not aside
I've tried to resist you everyway
With my foolish manly pride
Yet still within my lonely heart
There burns a constant fire
Which when I met you it did start
It's your love that I desire
So be not cold or cruel now
And let me suffer still
My life is possessed by your love
And I know it always will
So smile upon one who loves you
With a Love constant warm and true.

Love ~ 11

A mother loves an infant child
Our God he loves us all
Our friends love a friendly smile
Or if away our tele call
The birds they love the springtime
The skiers the fall of snow
The school kids love the summer time
The Squirrel the autumn's blow
The fish love open waters deep
Where they swim safe from harm
I love to nestle in deep sleep
My love here in your arms
I wonder how my life would be
If I didn't have you loving me.

Love ~ 12

Today the Sun is nice and hot
Tomorrow may bring rain
Yesterday 'twas snow we got
But in me my hearts the same
The seasons change all rapidly
Each day the weather change
But still you've remained constantly
With never a loveless change
And so I thought I'd say again
That you love are my life
You've brought joy removed pain
From my past cold lonely life
So here again may I promise you
For all my life True Love for you.

Racism ~ 1

Bitter life overrules me
It fills me with despair
There's no hope that I can see
Just sorrow everywhere
There's been but toil and labour
Ever since the days of old
When I was sold by you neighbour
For common silver or for gold
You have taken long my freedom
My lands my children and my home
Treated me like an animal dumb
And why I've never known
I do not understand what you crave
Why can't I live not as your Slave.

Racism ~ 2

You have not any item
That I would take from you
You can accomplish nothing
That given a chance I can't do
You enjoy your full freedom
And go upon your ways
Why can't I too enjoy some
For few of my wretched days
We breathe the same air daily
We eat food of one kind
We hold the same thoughts surely
So why can't I too live mine
Tell me if there's something I lack
We're so alike you white me black.

Racism ~ 3

You laze upon the beaches
Which I have made so clean
On Islands where in deepest reaches
My peoples blood I've seen
You try to take upon your skin
The very colour you condemn
Yet because mine comes from within
You treat me as no friend
You oil your bodies over
With tan producing cream
But should I touch you ever
You act like I'm unclean
What do you want white man
Please help me to understand.

Racism ~ 4

You lay with my sisters
They bear you children brown
You try then to resist her
And let your offsprings down
You jail me and you kill me
If with your kind I lay
Why is it good for you bad for me
Please explain me this I pray
I take her hand and press it
Warm and white upon mine black
But when she does remove it
No colour do I lack
And if it will not even stain
Why does my colour cause you pain.

Racism ~ 5

My children are so funny
When I see them thru your eyes
With skins of chocolate, milk or honey
And their multi-coloured eyes
With hair of straight or curly
Brunette or black or blonde
Yet they know I love them surely
My each and every one
If I can have this feeling
To a race that's done me ill
And keep your sister happy living
Why do you hate me still
I only want to live and love
Why can'– I even do this now.

Racism ~ 6

For four centuries of sorrow
I've waited for this day
When my life you wouldn't harrow
In my every step each day
I've lived in slums and ghettos
I've lived in fields and caves
I've been cast out where e'er I go
I've been beaten while your Slave
I've traversed o'er the oceans
In the slave ships you devised
Lying too packed to make a motion
Tortured by you and despised
Still I lived one day hoping
That your heart 'twould be opened.

Racism ~ 7

I've felt the weight of heavy chains
Which upon my feet you've placed
I've seen the trading blocks and pens
Where you auctioned off my race
I've read your published papers
Wherein rewards you gave
For return of my escapers
Who grew tired of being your Slave
My back is rough and welted
My breast brand-iron scarred
From the iron tipped whip you meted
Control each time I erred
Still my strength it did sustain
And let me live out all my pain.

Racism ~ 8

I showed you friendly faces
I've tried to be your friend
I've loved those of other races
Tried them all to understand
I've been your Slave and worker
I've been your man at war
I've grown to lose hates power
And to see you as a bore
But lastly I have learned now
That non-violence you condemn
And so thanks to Indifference now
I'm here to bring about your end
So prepare you for the fight
I may decide to kill you tonight.

Racism ~ 9

Your laws and institutions
I hold no fear of more
For your tortures and your prisons
I've felt them all before
Your guns and knives and ammo
I've used to fight your fights
For the freedom that I still don't know
Tho they were basic human rights
But it would be too easy
To conventionally end your life
You'd pass to death too quickly
To recall your past bigot's life
So I will slowly let you suffer
That each past day you will remember.

Racism ~ 10

For I have been crippled
I'll see you crippled too
I've been diseased and blinded
Your health and eyes shall be mine too
I've been beaten and broken
But your bones are just like mine
I've seen my people's spirit broken
Like you'll see yours in good time
I've felt the bliss of dying
As on your gallows I did lie
This I'll keep you from knowing
As so slowly I'll let you die
And when you think it is the end
I'll revive you and start again.

Racism ~ 11

I'll sit and watch your face
With regret deep down inside
That you suffer so for your race
Which so long held such pride
I'll think about your feelings too
And feel to set you free
I may even this attempt to do
If the last was left to me
But then when time shall open wide
And show history being turned
I'll know understanding deep inside
But let you live what I have learned
And even as you cry and yearn
I'll think as from your face I turn.

Racism ~ 12

Yes life is but a giant wheel
Which we are caught upon
We each should for the other feel
Before we move along
And since you in your better days
Did seek me to enslave
I'm sorry but this is my day
To help you to your grave
And tho I no longer love or hate
And ask not what is right
To be Black forever is my fate
While yours is to be White
Strange that things end this way
Together we could have all been great

Pollution ~ 1

Pollution is a heavy thing
That fills our every day
The air and sea and everything
In misty musky odor stay
Our birds we hunt no longer
Our fish we do not trap
'Cause they die of daily hunger
Or of some fast poisoning crap
Their feathers once all glitter
With hardly one being soiled
Now are waterproofed far better
With their thick coat of crude oil
Still production persists
As our wildlife vainly resists.

Pollution ~ 2

The sea the sea the garbage sea
The oil which on you float
You meant life and love to me
As I crossed you in that boat
Alas the boat it sprang a leak
The 'Captain' ordered "Pumps"
A million gallons of oil so bleak
Into your laps he dumped
Tho you tried your best to open out
The oil we did discard
To send it here and there about
You really tried so hard
But Sea you didn't master it
So your beaches try to absorb it.

Pollution ~ 3

On moonlit coral sands I sat
On many a lovely night
Wondering of the lovely mat
So warm so clean so white
But now alas just today's morn
As beachwards I did gaze
I saw in dismay yesterdays storm
Had destroyed my memories
For tho I live a thousand miles
Or two or maybe three
The oil had found our little Isle
Which once was home to me
And now my life is dull and grey
As birds and fish I see dead lay.

Pollution ~ 4

You say that this is progress
You'll clean it all up soon
But I can't see what you profess
When each night you hide the moon
You gave me warmth and shelter
You say from factories that are
But I find it hard to remember
When last I saw a star
You build and blast and pollute
Saying it soon will all be done
But I'm pale and sickly in truth
As each day you hide our Sun
How much longer can we wait
'Til your pollution our lives abate.

Pollution ~ 5

I smoke not, but I cough and choke
Each day I take a walk
My eyes burn like you they did poke
My throat's sore when I talk
My garden has had flowers bright
Before you did in mass spray
Some poison droplets in the night
To drive the bugs away
The bugs refused to be run
The flowers failed to grow
The beauty garden now is gone
But I shouldn't say 'I told you so'
That would be too radical of me
'Stead I wait for what you do to me.

Pollution ~ 6

My country 'twas of you
That birds and peoples sang
With Tropic breezes blowing thru
You gave pride unto our land
Our waters clean and open lay
A picture window bright
Now there's garbage on every bay
And nothing now looks right
A factory is spewing content
A million tons each day
Of oily sticky effluent
In our world's renown bay
But think of the money they've spent
Is all we hear from our Government.

Pollution ~ 7

We may be poor but healthy
We may not have too much
We cannot strive to be wealthy
If we must pollute each thing we touch
We see the greedy industry
Take all our choicest land
With no consideration of you and me
As they exploit our dear land
Soon we will be commercialized
Like the great and mighty nation
Living with masks o'er our eyes
To protect us from pollution
We must accept this as progress
Or worldly gains we won't possess.

Pollution ~ 8

Do not try to chide me
And please tell me no lies
I've seen polluted lands and seas
Which I did once pass by
I've held the birds all oily
I've heard the seal's death cry
So save your lies for some surely
Who has seen far less than I
I've worked within your factories
I've pumped your poisoned waste
I've smelled your stink distilleries
Left your pulp and paper mills in haste
We need to live in health
Even though it means less wealth.

Pollution ~ 9

Thank you for your autocar
Which takes us on our way
It drives us fast near or far
Closer to our graves each day
It takes our wages for gasoline
It takes our gold to insure
It pollutes our every air stream
It's habit forming with no cure
It kills upon our highways
Or in closed garages off the street
By brutal pain and crippling ways
Or fumes that smell so sweet
But who would be without one
The smart father of a young one.

Pollution ~ 10

The Sun today blinked its eye
Or so to us it seemed
Awakening with a dismal sigh
As from a restless dream
It caught a chance to happen to
To find a spot so clean
That its rays could shine thru
And by the world be seen
But people so unaccustomed
To its light they had become
That seeing it some were stunned
The rest did become quite dumb
Then we... we hid in deepest fear
Certain that the end was near.

Pollution ~ 11

Let's no longer treat this thing
As a joke or passing scene
It's time we sat and realized
Just what pollution means
It takes away our breathing
It fouls our eyes and mouth
It destroys natures balanced ending
And casts it's beauty out
It kills our air and water
For our productions sake
To the wildlife it's quick slaughter
On land or sea or lake
Yet we tolerate the makers
Who also are the profit takers.

Pollution ~ 12

Sorry we cannot feed you gull
When we ride upon this ship
Our washrooms remain in useless lull
For long periods every trip
We must do our part to protect
The environment from danger
While permission is given to eject
The pulpmill's waste into the water
The peoples a few thousand
Could not very much harm do
Compared with the thousand thousands
Of waste gallons daily the mills spew
But alas industry is king
And you and I don't mean a thing.

Life ~ 1

Life is a flame of tomorrow
An ember of yesterday
A smoke of some past sorrow
Or the warmth of love today
Life is the pitter-patter
Of tiny uncertain feet
Or the smile that egos flatter
When a love we chance to meet
Life is the falling rainbow
And the chilling icy snow
Life is the one thing we can't stop
No matter how hard we try to
Yet life it is worth living
If you enjoy getting and giving.

Life ~ 2

What causes the state of life
I wonder so many ways
What is the ultimate of life
Is what me doth truly amaze
Where do we go hereafter
Can life be continued still
Or is all our pain and laughter
Mere fantasies of our will
Will it be here at morning
Or evening when it will shine bright
The meaning for which we're waiting
The answer that will bring light
Ncy we pass on like a flower
While living is loving each other.

Life ~ 3

I chase a dream called life
But I find it doesn't answer
The questions of today's strife
The many problems that I ponder
It's just a dream I know
From which we must awaken
But when we do where do we go
And how much time has been taken
I do not claim to understand
Or even have a wild thought
Just what is this life's plan
Through which we all are brought
Like sheep innocent to slaughter
Knowing pain, peace, joy or laughter.

Life ~ 4

Yet on we go without an end
Like so many bits of flotsam
Across timeless sea without end
Hoping for answers from someone
Still knowing well our time is nigh
When we too must pass out yonder
Going to some outer region high
Moving into some calm blue wonder
Or living yet another time
Another life of peace and beauty
To live like in some poets rhyme
Forever doing to the world our duty
Living is but a state of mind
A state we all should try to find.

Life ~ 5

If death is the end of living
Then take death and leave me life
If love is the art of existing
May my soul ne'er know strife
If pain is a point of feeling
To prove that I am alive
Then do to me pain for I'm willing
To at life's far reaches arrive
Take care tho in all you may do
That be heart or body removed
Give me back when you're thru
Life... that it may be improved
For without life I am nothing
But in life I always am something.

Life ~ 6

Faces all around me stare
At me as at a freak
With curious questions they don't care
What evil of me they speak
Trying to elate to my esteem
Or pull me to their level
I'm treated as one who can redeem
Or I'm scorned as an evil devil
My time 's short, thus I try
Their presence to out-tune
And live my life just passing by
Them, like old garbage strewn
No longer will they my life dictate
No more to rule or govern my fate.

Life ~ 7

So like a tiny baby fair
You lay upon the bed
With the pillow painted by your hair
In gold, black, brown or red
Your face enveloped in between
The curls that softly lie
Brings memories back of a dream
When life held you and I
Yet glancing now around the place
I see but the empty wall
Which held the picture of your face
Before I lost my all
Yes life in death took you from me
While dead in life is how I be.

Life ~ 8

Yesterday you were born
And grew up fast today
But I pray that the early morn
Won't take you e'er away
Your laughter and smile
Your small warm caress
Has touched me inside
With your warm tenderness
I fear for naught else now
But what tomorrow it may bring
For to me you are life love
You're my Summer and my Spring
So may the bleak Winter's cold
Ne'er rest long 'gainst your door.

Life ~ 9

My lines and all my verses
I try to use to show
The pains, sorrows and abuses
Which I did so often know
To help you understand dear
That life is full of woe
To comfort you when I'm not near
To assist where'er you go
To bring to eye and mind too
The beauty of life's way
To help you appreciate anew
The life you live today
With hopes of bright tomorrows
When you will know no sorrows.

Life ~ 10

Walking down a street we meet
That's life that's life
Years have passed pasts delete
That's life that's life
Seeing man at woman glance
Seeing birds aflying round
Seeing babies take a chance
Seeing life and all its sounds
That's life that's life
That's life as I have known it
That's life that's life
But ne'er would I change it
For of all the things I've had
Life still is really not too bad.

Life ~ 11

Forgive me for spoiling your life
In a way you can't see
It meant to give you happiness bright
It was not meant to be
I tried to assist and amend
Your lone broken dreams
But you thought I did but pretend
And it was only a scheme
I'm sorry life's sometimes this way
I guess you've heard that before
But please forgive me someday
And then hate me no more
Content I'll remain tho apart
Happy I once lived in your heart.

Life ~ 12

What a cloudy misty day
One wonders what is wrong
The world lies in dismal grey
The birds they sing no song
The waters lie so calm
The winds don't even blow
But still we feel no alarm
For we're living free we know
We have no chains to bind
We have no axe to grind
We have a life let's live it
Find love leave hate behind
For even in its dismal way
The world is beautiful today.

Toronto's Street

I walked along a lonely street
My heart held in my hand
I sought here but companionship
One who would understand
I saw my past go hurried by
I saw olden dreams again
I thought for just one moment short
I'd found my long lost friend
But as I walked in lone despair
Accepting finally that it's gone
The past becomes a reality
As by me you hurried on
Silently without a word of recognition
I alone on Toronto's street sans anticipation

Thank You

Thank you for your interest
In the words I to you sent
Of the deepest thoughts I possess
Things by which this world is rent
In past, present or future
You too may come upon
A scene such as I picture
Before your life is gone
I hope that by my sorrows
Or hardship and woe you'll find
Many a warm and bright tomorrow
By avoiding mistakes of mine
Then my talent will bear fruitfully
Employed by the help you get from me

<u>Other Collections by This Author:</u>

A Poet's Ebb And Flow

... and Touches Of Nature

In The Middle of Believe There's A Lie

Inside A Heart

Judge Me Not Without A Trial

Legends, Lives & Loves Along the Inside Passage

Love... Life's Illusive Zenith

Love's Reflections

Only Children Of The Universe Are We

Step Scenes Of Life

That We Too Free May Live

~ ~

For more information go to:

w w w . d n c s i t e . c a

~ ~

www.ingramcontent.com/pod-product-compliance
Lightning Source LLC
Chambersburg PA
CBHW021346090426
42742CB00008B/761